*Monty Don &
Derry Moore*

*Great
Gardens
of Italy*

Quadrille
PUBLISHING

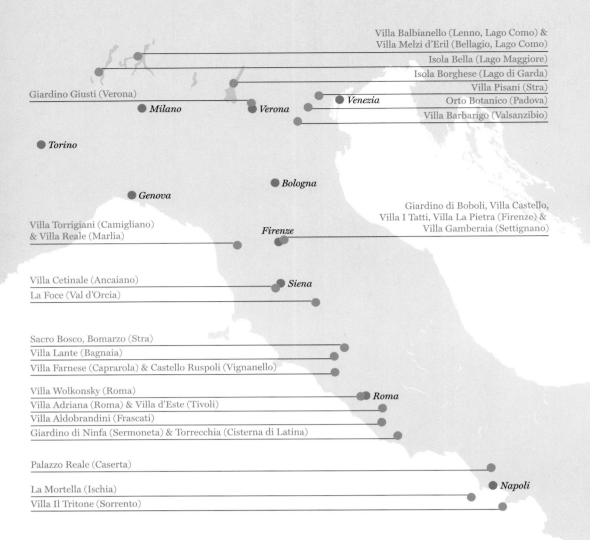

Villa Balbianello (Lenno, Lago Como) &
Villa Melzi d'Eril (Bellagio, Lago Como)

Isola Bella (Lago Maggiore)

Isola Borghese (Lago di Garda)

Villa Pisani (Stra)

Orto Botanico (Padova)

Villa Barbarigo (Valsanzibio)

Giardino Giusti (Verona)

Milano

Verona

Venezia

Torino

Bologna

Genova

Giardino di Boboli, Villa Castello,
Villa I Tatti, Villa La Pietra (Firenze) &
Villa Gamberaia (Settignano)

Villa Torrigiani (Camigliano)
& Villa Reale (Marlia)

Firenze

Villa Cetinale (Ancaiano)

La Foce (Val d'Orcia)

Siena

Sacro Bosco, Bomarzo (Stra)

Villa Lante (Bagnaia)

Villa Farnese (Caprarola) & Castello Ruspoli (Vignanello)

Villa Wolkonsky (Roma)

Villa Adriana (Roma) & Villa d'Este (Tivoli)

Villa Aldobrandini (Frascati)

Giardino di Ninfa (Sermoneta) & Torrecchia (Cisterna di Latina)

Roma

Palazzo Reale (Caserta)

La Mortella (Ischia)

Villa Il Tritone (Sorrento)

Napoli

A map of the gardens in this book. Although they were chosen without any particular desire to create an even geographical spread and inevitably tend to cluster around the great cities, they do cover a large part of the country and were visited as a meandering journey from south to north.

Page 1: The stone hounds of Villa Gamberaia turn their back on the spectacular view across the Tuscan countryside towards Florence, faithfully watching over the villa and its garden.
Page 2: Formal clipped hedges and trees at Villa I Tatti create abstract , extremely modern, green layers of texture, structure and line. The garden in the village of Settignano, outside Florence, was made by Cecil Pinsent and Geoffrey Scott between 1909 and 1920 for the art dealer Bernard Berenson. It was the first garden either had ever attempted to make and was hugely influential in promoting an Italianate, neo-Renaissance style.

6 Introduction

10 Naples
14 Villa Il Tritone, Sorrento
20 Palazzo Reale, Caserta
26 La Mortella, Ischia

32 Rome
36 Giardino de Ninfa, Sermoneta
46 Torrecchia, Cisterna di Latina
50 Villa Adriana, Roma
54 Villa d'Este, Tivoli
64 Villa Aldobrandini, Frascati
72 Villa Wolkonsky, Roma

76 Viterbo
80 Villa Farnese, Caprarola
88 Villa Lante, Bagnaia
96 Castello Ruspoli, Vignanello
100 Sacro Bosco, Bomarzo

104 Tuscany
108 Villa Castello, Firenze
114 Giardino di Boboli, Firenze
122 Villa Gamberaia, Settignano
130 Villa La Pietra, Firenze
134 Villa I Tatti, Firenze
138 La Foce, Val d'Orcia
144 Villa Cetinale, Siena
148 Villa Torrigiani, Camigliano
156 Villa Reale, Marlia

162 Veneto
166 Orto Botanico, Padova
170 Villa Barbarigo, Valsanzibio
178 Villa Pisani, Stra
184 Giardino Giusti, Verona

192 The Lakes
196 Villa Balbianello, Lenno
202 Isola Borghese, Lago di Garda
206 Villa Melzi d'Eril, Bellagio
210 Isola Bella, Lago Maggiore

218 Chronology
220 Index
224 Acknowledgements

Introduction

Monty Don

My introduction to Italy was a two-week visit to Venice thirty years ago and although I have returned many times since, for the most part saw tantalisingly few gardens. Tantalising because the ones that I did see inspired me greatly. A few years ago I made a round-the-world trip visiting gardens and whilst that was extraordinary and fascinating I realised that I longed to make a much less frenetic journey concentrating on the gardens of just one country, giving them the time that I needed to absorb them. There was never any doubt in my mind what that one country might be and almost as soon as I had finished my round-the-world marathon garden tour I started making plans to make a series of slow trips to Italy. Various events meant that this had to wait a couple of years but there was no harm in that. I read about Italian gardens, thought about them and gardened.

My own garden is greatly influenced by Italian gardens almost despite itself because in many ways the setting and my background could not be more conventionally British. Twenty years ago I read Jellicoe and Shepherd's *Italian Gardens of the Renaissance* and it made a powerful impression on me. I was particularly struck by the simple notion of learning a garden by measuring it out, using one's body as measurement – a pace, a step, a handspan – and then drawing it up. This is inevitably a slow, intimate process of getting to know a garden like a body. It is almost the exact opposite of the fast, glib gratification that inevitably accompanies quick visits with instant analysis and judgements. This simple, slow, patient way of taking in any garden seemed to be a likelier key to understanding it and getting the most from it.

I love the organisation of space through hedges, topiary, landscaping and buildings, love the sculptural possibilities in plants and the horticultural settings for sculpture. Unlike Geoffrey Jellicoe, I adore individual plants and gain deep satisfaction from growing them, but the very British ideal of the garden as a botanical showcase of rarities or collection of plants has always rather bored me. What you do, rather than what you do it with, has always seemed the really interesting thing about a garden and the Italian garden where extreme formality merges into abstraction of the most modern kind has always seemed much more exciting and interesting.

Also the more that I garden the more I revere green. In Italy's parched summer landscape the green patterns of box, yew, bay or holm oak have a strength and cool reassurance. In the brown and grey bleakness of a northern winter green lifts the gloom and is an affirmation of life whilst everything above ground is shrivelling and dying back. But it is a gross oversimplification to think that even the most formal Italian garden was devoid of colour or flowers. The Italianate of the turn of the nineteenth and twentieth centuries fostered that belief, not least by re-creating superb pure green gardens such as the parterres at Caprarola or the work of Cecil Pinsent at I Tatti or La Foce. But Cosimo Medici, who made what is now the oldest surviving Renaissance garden at Villa Castello, was a great botanist, as were his successors. The founding of the great botanical gardens at Padua and Pisa within months of each other testifies to the fascination with plants of all kinds at the same time as some of the most famous formal gardens in history were being made such.

Italian gardens both illustrate and bring to life history and are made from it as much as any building. To understand the garden you have to know its story. There is no better way of delving into the mind and lives of the names that criss-cross Italian history than walking in the shade of their gardens, smelling their plants and hearing the water flow that they also listened to.

Whilst Italian history is mapped out in its gardens the present, with a few exceptions that prove the rule, is conspicuously absent. As I visited more and more Italian gardens I realised that the popular culture of gardening has almost disappeared from modern Italy. Head gardeners in private gardens are highly unlikely to be Italian. I asked one British head gardener if he had trouble recruiting local staff. "It is almost impossible," he said. "You only consider becoming a gardener in Italy if you are unable to do any other kind of work." This means that most state gardens are poorly run, badly maintained and staff relationships

Opposite top: Classical remains on the Appenine Hill above the Forum. The stone pines of Rome define the city's skyline although in fact the majority were planted under the enthusiastic promotion by the fascist government of the 1920s and '30s.

Opposite bottom: The terrace of The Hundred Fountains at Villa d'Este at Tivoli, just outside Rome. Water was the key to all great gardens of the Renaissance and people went to huge expense to divert and channel it into their gardens. Once there it was manipulated into astonishing performances and displays.

constantly simmer at the edge of unrest. It is an unhappy situation which could become disastrous for some of the greatest gardens in the world.

On the other hand Italian garden historians and conservationists are as good as any in the world. They have a deep and enlightened understanding of the history and context of their gardens which are often beautifully restored with great historical sensitivity. Yet it is telling that it would never cross the mind of any of these specialists to get their hands dirty and actually garden themselves. The two worlds are not so much separate as mutually exclusive.

The reason for this is, I think, tied to Italy's very recent past. Until the Second World War the countryside was a place of hardship, often real poverty and an almost feudal relationship between landowners and tenants. Mussolini's fascists started the process away from this, improving conditions and handing land to tenants but the fascist connotations that go with that and the total upheaval of the war meant that by 1960 Italy was socially reinventing itself as a commercial, industrial state. Manual work was redolent of impoverished, tied labour, even in the garden.

Nothing could be further from the British reverence for the act of gardening and mastery of its skills. But substitute food for gardening in the two cultures and you approach a better understanding. The sensuous pleasure in process and every detail that the British instinctively apply to their gardens is how the Italians treat every meal. My Italian friends do not question just the precise ingredients of each dish, but also its provenance and how exactly it was to be prepared and cooked. More often than not these are dishes that they have eaten countless times before and frequently in that very restaurant and the boundaries between what they eat at home and in restaurants are blurred to the point of being indistinguishable. This is almost the exact opposite of the average British experience where the enjoyment of being 'treated' by a professional chef rather than a common cook is the ideal, and the more mystery in the process and the further removed from everyday eating, generally the better it is received. This – at once removed – is how the Italians best enjoy their gardens.

British gardens are based upon an institutionalised nostalgia and reverence for the countryside. Italian culture, however, has always been based around cities. Yet their gardens have long been seen as a retreat from city life. This makes them an anomaly. Medieval gardens were essentially practical places for growing herbs and fruit that were enclosed, beautiful and sometimes private but drawing from classical sources, particularly the writings of Ovid and Pliny, the Renaissance adopted and developed this idea of the garden as a beautiful retreat. To create a beautiful garden in the middle of a magnificent landscape was to tame nature and introduce culture – hence the presence of sculpture and buildings on a grand scale as well as the formality of avenues, parterres, highly controlled water features and entertainments. Order, control and sophistication were delightful precisely because they were *not* the natural landscape. It took until the nineteenth century for the 'English' garden – loose, unstructured and park-like – to become popular in Italy.

Visiting gardens is one of the best ways of getting to know a country. I use public transport wherever possible, which in Italy is made easy by the largely excellent train system. It is the best way to see the countryside and to watch and listen to local people. It is a slow process but gardens cannot be hurried. They often take a while to reveal themselves. You have to deal with – and accept – the weather and the season. I paid very few of these gardens just one visit. Some I returned to three or four times. Every time was different. Every time added something new.

There have been plenty of good academic books written about Italian gardens, many of which I have used in my research. My choice and description of gardens is personal and very subjective. If the combination of the text and Derry Moore's wonderful pictures provokes the reader to visit some of them and then violently disagree with my account then so much the better. And if the visitor has half as much fun in doing so as I did then they are in for a richly rewarding time.

Opposite top: The far end of the bowling alley at Villa Gamberaia. Villa Gamberaia has survived as a huge influence on twentieth-century garden makers because, despite its grandeur, it is on a domestic scale.

Opposite bottom: A section of the vast parterre at Castello Ruspoli. There is nothing domestic about any part of Castello Ruspoli but the parterre, made in the first decade of the seventeenth century, remains unchanged and in the same family that made it.

Naples

For anyone fed upon stories of Naples as a kind of lawless urban jungle with streets piled with rubbish, robbers and muggers spotting every possible giveaway of the wealthy tourist and traffic that reduces life expectancy by decades, then the first visit comes as a profound shock. Not because of the farcically chaotic journey from the airport or because of the grafitti that seems to deface every statue and building, but because it is one of the most beautiful cities in the world. There is no other city in Italy that I would rather spend a few days in as a tourist.

Rather than being the slightly seedy, corrupt place that northern Europeans might conjure it has, since its Greek origins in the eighth century BC, been a grand and important city. Until the middle of the nineteenth century it was by far the biggest city in Italy, capital of a kingdom that stretched from Sicily in the south as far as the Abruzzo region north of Rome.

But there are two abiding images of Naples that remain with me. The first is of Pepino and his 85-year-old mother on their four-hectare smallholding set on the terraced slopes of an old crater in the Fuorigrotta region in the northwest of the city. Pepino showed me the modified ski lift that he uses to pull kit and crates of produce up and down the hillside that his 85-year-old mother effortlessly walked up. Pepino feeds his extended family well with a small vineyard, orchard, chickens and rabbits and vegetables and there is income enough from the sales of the surplus for a new house and a comfortable, if simple, life. I had lunch with them and the pasta with fresh peas, bacon and lemon was as good as anything I have ever eaten – which is not to say that the other six courses were not heavenly too – and every scrap, including the white, rose and red wine, all from their terraces above the house.

As we walked round I asked him what was the turnaround before a terrace could be replanted with the same crop? "Eighty to a hundred years," he said. I thought I'd misheard. Eight to ten years? A pretty long, but healthy, rotation. But the extra noughts were really there. Eighty to a hundred years! Incredible! How did he know or remember the

Looking out into the Mediterranean from Villa San Michele on Capri. There is a quality of light around the coast from the Bay of Naples, its islands such as Ischia and Capri and down the Amalfi coast, that is fresher, brighter and more liberating than anywhere else in Italy.

rotation pattern? Was there a record? He shook his head. "My mother tell me." How did she know? "Her mother told her." And so it had gone for hundreds of years. The connection to the soil and the food it produces was umbilical and as personal as the ties of blood. I looked out with Pepino over the old volcanic crater that last erupted two millennia ago although Solfatara bubbles and threatens. The city jostled and sprawled hard against his land. If he sold up he could make a fortune. Would he consider it? He laughed. "I have everything I need here," he said. "Everything."

The other image is less romantic. I had taken the train to Rome (incredibly fast and efficient, less than one hour door to door) for the day and returned to have dinner with the film crew I was working with. I got a call to say dinner was delayed because they were at the police station. Their van had been halted in traffic by a scooter that drew across in front of them. At the same time two other scooters drew up behind the van. One rider got off, opened the rear doors, jumped in, stole tens of thousands of pounds worth of kit and sped off almost before anyone had registered what had happened.

Experiences like this do not diminish the architectural beauty of Naples or devalue the sun, sea and easy friendliness of the people. Life might be rather anarchic but it is also good. Simple food is cheap and delicious – this is the home of pasta and tomato sauce, with the local San Marzano tomato proudly proclaimed the best in the world – and lemons they claim to be second to none although there is intense local rivalry with those of Amalfi an hour or two round the rocky corner. Perhaps less expected but astonishingly beautiful are the fabulous chestnut coppices of the hillside between the bay of Naples and Salerno, with the 30-foot bare stems cut by the hundreds of thousands to provide structure to support the shading for the lemon groves. For a gardener, to see that cycle of growth, harvest and skilful use to create another harvest carrying on into the twenty-first century has a deep power and resonance.

Looking out across the Bay of Naples from Villa Il Tritone at Sorrento towards Mount Vesuvius. Pompeii is just to the right, on the shoreline, and the tsunami that followed the eruption of 79AD swept across the bay and submerged the original villa.

Naples

I arrived in Sorrento in the dark having driven round to the far side of the Bay of Naples to the last promontory before Capri with Vesuvius behind me all the way. "You will wake to see the mountain," the receptionist said and gave me a room looking out over the sea. Every Italian hotel will dutifully close windows, shutters and curtains as part of preparing the room for the night, regardless of weather or view, so I duly opened everything as wide as it would go so the mountain would be framed in the window and slept. I was woken by a blast on a ship's hooter and the prow of a vast cruising ship sliding across the window before noisily dropping anchor just off shore. Vesuvius was sulking in the mist and not coming out to play.

What I could see as I ate my breakfast outside was Villa Il Tritone sitting right on the edge of the cliffs with a dense outcrop of trees behind it which were, I later realised, the garden. From a little closer, down in the harbour where the boats bring in fish rather than cruisers, it looks like a fortified castle and the trees are all shaped and pruned. Every bit of it is well under control. The villa – and its garden – was originally a lot lower, right down at and below sea level. There was a villa on the site that belonged to the man who built the Pantheon in Rome, Augustus's grandson Marcus Vipsanius Agrippa, before it was washed away by the tsunami that followed the great eruption of Vesuvius in 79AD. The footings of the villa can still be glimpsed under the water if you peer down over the walls that extend the cliff face, but marble columns and various other artefacts from that original building, some Egyptian and already a thousand years old when the waves buried them, were discovered in the past hundred years and are now in the garden.

In the thirteenth century a convent for the nuns of St Clare was built there before the Turks came through, raping and pillaging and leaving it in ruins. This was eventually followed by a monastery until in the nineteenth century it was bought by a Baron Labonia who built the villa and made the first garden. Il Tritone was then purchased by William Waldorf Astor in 1905. Astor came from a wealthy New York family, was formerly the U.S. ambassador in Rome before

becoming a British citizen and eventually a viscount and owner of Hever Castle in Kent and Cliveden in Buckinghamshire. He enlarged the grounds and much of the existing garden was laid out by him. Astor loved the place and used it as a retreat from politics, diplomacy and the hurly-burly of Rome. The modern garden still feels like a retreat and, despite being perched so prominently on the bay, remains completely private.

It was bought in 1973 by Mariano and Rita Pane and Rita met me and showed me round the garden. It is dominated by two things – the view out and shelter from sunlight and the view in. The view out with its intensely blue sea and sky and, at last, the hint of Vesuvius flirting with the mist, is framed so that it becomes distilled. The framing comes partly from the planting, particularly the series of covered walks, but principally by a wall designed by Harold Peto, the designer hired by Astor when he bought the garden. Peto built the wall to screen off the view, revealing it in a series of shuttered windows, using colonnades, balustrades and sculptures collected by Labonia and Astor. The result is a kind of long gallery with windows on the sea, each opening a sapphire jewel set in its frame, intensified and condensed. It is extraordinarily powerful. It also serves to stop the likes of me having my breakfast – and as the day progresses, hundreds more – looking up and watching us looking down. The privacy to see but not be seen has always been the prerogative of the rich and powerful ever since the first tower was built.

The garden is labyrinthine in its use of covered paths and walkways, cleverly designed to make the most of the space, which is probably only a couple of acres. It seems much larger. The paths have a lattice of chestnut poles over them, one covered by a wisteria, the racemes hanging low, another with a truly enormous banksia rose, the tiny lemon flowers still out when I was there at the end of April, and the combination of the slightly wonky poles and the tracery of the rose stems and the filigree of leaves was like an enormous stained glass window. The light filtered down to the paths, richly green with moss. A green medley of plants fringes the walks – cycads and cypress, palms and pines and unclipped box. It is lush, dense, intense and deliciously cool. In spring that coolness was tempered by the bright light at the end of each path but in high summer it must be a blessed relief.

There are enormous pots everywhere and yellow marble dredged up from the sea. Blank-eyed busts set their best profile silhouetted against the horizon. The history is very present in the garden, layered like geology right down to the seabed far below.

In front of the villa is the one formal piece of garden with sunken beds of lavender in great blocks, roses, a cistern, raised lily pond with the unlikely backdrop of a bank of cycads and everywhere the sense of plants slowly taking their anarchic route to a dissolving, untrammelled greenness. It is lovely.

In the lower garden the moss becomes positively architectural strewn with camellia petals as naturally arch as a Japanese tea garden. I take my shoes and socks off and soak up the cool from the peachy fuzz of the moss through the soles of my feet.

Before I left Rita gave me lunch. I record it for you in every detail because it was – eaten outside on a patio over the now cloudless bay with Vesuvius dramatically present, half-performance half-threat – as good a meal as I have ever known and a meal, with commonplace ingredients, which could not possibly be replicated anywhere in the world save within ten miles of that garden. We started with pasta with tomato (San Marzano, of course, the prince of tomatoes in Naples), chilli and shrimps from one of the boats below. Not knowing what, if anything, was to follow I accepted the second helping on the basis that it was completely delicious and what the hell, it would have been rude to say no. Then followed a sea bass cooked with lemon and oil: fish from the sea below and oil and lemon from the hillside running down to the water. The wine was light, white, from a vineyard round the corner. Other than the superbly cooked fish, just baked in foil, the lemon was laugh-out-loud good because, as Rita explained, "The lemons from Sorrento are the best in the world. It is a fact. And to get the best from them you must pick and use them the same day." We had a salad of chicory and rocket – both gathered wild from the hillside; a whole, delicately creamy local mozzarella served in a figure of eight, and made from cow's milk rather than buffalo; and finally a plate of biscuits. These looked charming but unexceptional, little sandwiches of pastry with lemon-flavoured ricotta cheese filling them. They were served with Rita's home-made lemoncello. "Take one, please. Take two." I bit in. Angels sang. Stars shot through the universe tumbling for joy. I have never known such a clean intensity in the mouth. So, exercising all the restraint I could muster and only to be polite, you understand, I only ate five biscuits and only had the two glasses of lemoncello.

Vesuvius dominates the view but is often hidden in mist. It appeared for just an hour or so when I visited. The garden is full of remains from the Roman villa, like the column that the urn stands on, dredged from the seabed.

The paths at Il Tritone are covered by a lattice made from long poles, cut from nearby chestnut coppice, which provide shade and support, in this case for a huge Banksia rose. These moss-carpeted tunnels burrow into the garden, its large collection of ferns and cycads both relishing and increasing the cool shade.

Above: Much of the charm of Il Tritone comes from the balance between formality, with a huge number of pots, urns and sculptures, and a stylish scruffiness. Moss is allowed to creep and branches to lean.

Opposite top: In front of the villa is a formal piece of garden with sunken beds of lavender planted and cut in great blocks. A raised cistern at the end is a lily pond – the flowers only revealed when you stand above it. Despite the formal layout there is everywhere the sense of plants slowly taking their anarchic route.

Opposite bottom: The view out towards Naples is deliberately distilled and condensed within frames. The garden designer Harold Peto was hired by William Waldorf Astor when he bought the garden in 1905 and he built the wall along the garden's edge above the bay to screen off the view, revealing it in a series of shuttered windows, incorporating colonnades, balustrades and stonework from the original villa destroyed at the same time as Pompeii.

La Mortella was made on the site of an
old quarry and the lower section, the
Valley Garden, has a microclimate where
Susana Walton's exuberant and eclectic
mix of plants thrive despite being a dry,
rocky site before she began planting.
Tree ferns, *Cyathera cooperi*, form a
leafy umbrella over the damp garden.

Looking back down the main rill (made
from terracotta roofing tiles), this is a
deliberate nod towards the great garden
at the Alhambra in Granada, Spain.
On the left is one of the many cycads
that add a tropical, not to say surreal,
feel to this Mediterranean garden.

The natural flora of the hillside still remains in a few parts of the garden and is made up of scrubby holm oak and olives with an understorey of the myrtle growing between the rocks that give the garden its name. ('Le Mortelle' is Neapolitan dialect for myrtle.)

The difference between the hillside and the Valley Garden, just a hundred metres away, is astonishing. The area around the main pond designed by Russell Page is known as the Rainforest and defies all the limitations that a less exuberantly determined spirit than Susana Walton might have succumbed to.

Rome

No other city throngs like Rome. Get into the wrong place at the wrong time of day and every excursion involves pushing through dense crowds. But get up early, avoid the summer months, public holidays or obvious tourist traps and no other city is such a pleasure simply to stroll around. I visited Rome on over half a dozen occasions during the process of writing this book but before I began I spent a week just walking the streets. It was a joy. I love the way that a major capital city can have artisan workshops and hardware stores in a side street right in the heart of impossibly venerable buildings and the fanciest of shops. For all its tourists it is a city that is lived in and used with the same possessiveness and pride of its localities as any provincial town.

Mind you, the traffic is bonkers. There is nowhere to park. If ever a modern city lent itself to reducing or freeing itself from the tyranny of the car it is Rome. But given the Italian deep love for cars it will take more than a generalised concern over carbon emissions to change this. The problem is that so much of its treasures are underground. The classical remains in Rome are staggering – and a walk round the Forum at 8A.M. on a Sunday morning is the best way to see them – but they are the tip of a subterranean iceberg. Put a spade in the ground and you have an archeological dig so it has the most limited underground system of any major European city and few multistorey car parks.

Of course the classical remains of the Forum, Colosseum and thousands of structures and buildings across the city, such as the aqueduct that runs through the garden of the British Embassy at Villa Wolkonsky, provoked and inspired the Renaissance having been ignored or neglected throughout the whole of the Middle Ages. Some of the inspiration was architectural, some based upon the humanism of the body as seen in the sculpture, some was brutally practical as thousands of tons of stone were robbed to provide building material. But the relationship with its physical classical past has remained central – and problematic – ever since.

In the light of a summer's evening the old kitchens of Villa Aldobrandini show all the charm of the huge villa and estate allowed to become slightly faded and run down, but retaining the confidence of a private and well-used home.

So you walk. Visit the Borghese Gardens – one of the best public parks in the world – taking a guided tour (only in French) around the gardens of Villa Medici or walking across to the other side to see the Etruscan collection in Villa Giulia and its small but perfect garden. The Orto Botanico lays no claims to be the best botanic garden in Italy, let alone the world, but it has real charm. My Roman friends scorn the Trastevere as being wholly taken over by Americans but it is beautiful, the restaurants good and the Botanical Garden rounds off a gentle wander round its streets perfectly.

High above Trastevere, across the river on the Aventine Hill, is the Garden of the Order of the Knights of Malta. To get into it you have to gain special permission and enter a thick wooden door that few get beyond. But the best of the garden can be seen from outside, peering with one eye to the keyhole. This exactly frames the Dome of St Peter's so that it fills the eye. In reality it is cunningly focused by a long tunnel of bay, at the end of which it appears no more than a small bump on an unremarkable, jumbled cityscape. But it is deliberately representing St Peter's – and the papacy – as the ultimate goal on any ambitious family's horizon, and the sixteenth century in particular seethed with ambitious cardinals prepared to do anything to occupy St Peter's. These cardinals and the great dynasties such as the Medici, Borghese, Borgia, Aldobrandini, Farnese and Orsini families all had villas and palaces in the city but the gardens that they made in their summer palaces at Frascati, Tivoli and a little further afield around Viterbo produced a crop of gardens in the second half of the sixteenth century that are some of the great treasures of the world. And all were driven by that blinkered vision you see through the keyhole in Piazza dei Cavalieri di Malta. Visit St Peter's Square on a Sunday morning as the reverential queues form in their tourists clothes and the nuns line up to be photographed whilst the service is relayed on two enormous screens, you can still feel that magnetic power pulsing out from the Vatican.

Roses underplanted beneath olives pruned to accentuate and celebrate the scrawny hieroglyphics of their branches at Villa Landriana, forty kilometres south of Rome. The twenty-five acre garden was designed by Russell Page and has over five hundred different varieties of rose.

Rome

For a thousand years Ninfa was a busy town on the main road from Rome to Naples until 1381 when it was sacked by mercenaries and the remaining inhabitants, much reduced by plague and riddled with malaria from the surrounding marshes, abandoned it. Ninfa was an important place, to the extent that Pope Alexander II was crowned there in September 1159. At its early fourteenth-century peak before the Black Death ripped through Europe, it had a castle, seven churches, fourteen towers, a town hall, mills, 150 houses and around two thousand inhabitants – all of which made it a substantial town. Then for six centuries it lay abandoned and great trees grew amongst the fallen roofs and the buildings were submerged like sunken wrecks beneath the undergrowth.

But the Caetani family, who had been given it by Pope Boniface VIII in 1297, never relinquished it and could afford to keep it as a curiosity, neither forgotten nor abandoned but lying low. The town is set on the edge of marshy land, backed by mountains, so there were easier places to build or make roads and fields. Ninfa waited like a dormant seed in the ground.

The transformation into a garden began in the early twentieth century under the guidance of Prince Galassio Caetani, when he began clearing the undergrowth and shoring up the ruins. From the first he seems to have done so with a careful, almost tender touch that remains the essence of the garden to this day. He restored the castle and the town hall and surveyed the entire street system.

Galassio was no gardener but his work on the structure is as crucial as any of the subsequent plantings. There is no point where the stone of buildings or the vegetation growing up through, round and against it can separately define the garden. Its seamless integration with the decay of the buildings and the growth of the plants nurture each other combining to make a present of profound intensity.

Galassio did plant trees, most notably the avenue of cypresses that line the Via Romana, but also pines and oaks, cedars and *Magnolia grandiflora*. They are an essential element of the modern garden although it seems his main motive was privacy. I have seen a photograph of the garden in the 1920s from the top of the tower and it is a bare, open site dotted with broken buildings. The trees clothe it.

Galassio died a bachelor and the garden as we see it now was taken onto its next stage by his brother Roffredo and sister-in-law Marguerite although in fact he left the garden to their son Camillo. Roffredo did much work on the water courses but Marguerite began to plant lavishly. The fact that she herself worked in the garden, getting her wealthy hands dirty, was as un-Italian then as it is now. This hands-on affinity is part of what makes Ninfa great. The Caetani connection is real and Lauro Marchetti, the current curator for the Caetani Trust, shares that deep, visceral love for the place. Despite her practical, direct involvement in the garden, all the accounts of Marguerite's Ninfa are of an etherial, remote place cut off from the rest of the world as if in a beautiful bubble. It still has something of that quality.

Marguerite planted hundreds of roses, many of which are still there. Ninfa becomes roses better than anywhere else, whether they dip down from the branches of an oak, lean against the crumbling masonry or climb to the top of one of the cypresses. It is as though while visiting Ninfa when the roses are in full bloom you realise for the first time their full scope. A door of perception is cleansed.

Camillo was killed in the Second World War and it was his sister, Leila who really expanded Ninfa into its modern state. She and her English husband Hubert Howard took over the care of the garden and estate. Although they had no children of their own they became informal guardians to Lauro Marchetti, the youngest son of the steward, from the age of eight. Now in his sixties, Lauro grew up in the garden and knows every plant and every inch of it. Nothing is accidental or unconsidered and yet as much as possible is allowed to be. The intimacy that every visitor experiences goes back to that intensely personal care.

Visiting Ninfa is a shock. Nothing prepares for it. This garden is unlike any other in type, scale and components. Plenty are bigger, plenty also include ruins, plenty have lovely rivers running through them and plenty have parts that manipulate the same kind of sensitivity to structure and plants sharing the same space, but none are so breathtakingly beautiful. Ninfa is the most romantic garden in the world and contains as much beauty as any visit can bear.

Some gardens wear their history like a pennant. They seem to strut down the centuries like a model on the catwalk, fanfares heralding their seasonal displays. Ninfa's history is hidden in the undergrowth, glimpsed through the branches before it slips away. And because everything is suggested and only partially revealed, no other garden is so riven through with ghosts than Ninfa, the town that died and regrew as a garden. The pathways are streets where Roman legions marched and drunkards brawled, and the roses climb up bell towers and city walls, mulched by history.

The touch is light. Weeds are carefully left growing in the walls and compost heaps made inside buildings whilst stacks of bamboos lean against a doorway where a door last hung six hundred years before. A bonfire leaks threads of smoke in the clearing behind the ragged gable of a church. There is almost a delicate sense of preserving the anarchy of the ruin and loss, whilst the fabric is zealously and expensively protected. It is a brilliantly balanced act. All the memories remain and, as you lose your urgent, enquiring eye and let the garden come slowly to you, the ghosts appear. No garden is more haunted. No garden more easy with its past.

Water runs through it like quicksilver. Some of the minor watery details like where one stream crosses another are clever and beautiful, and the way that all the water is so urgent and quick, moving in narrow grass-edged rills is special and exciting. But that is only when set against what is to come and when you move to the river and the buildings all this is transcended. Ninfa is at its best along the banks of the river that pours through the garden like the first and freshest snowmelt, coming in fact from the hills above the garden and especially from a spring below the lake that feeds into it at the rate of over a thousand litres a second. The garden is charged by this racing, crystal-pure energy.

Some of the history can only be guessed at but there are points where details give Ninfa's distant past a crisp edge. On the Ponte del Macello, crossing the river by the town wall, there is an open square vent over one of its twin arches. The story is that this was made so that butchers could bring meat up the river to the town during times of plague and baskets would be lowered down from the bridge to the boats below, and the meat drawn up through the holes. Stand there today and you can feel the hempen rope in your hands, hear it rasp against the stone and catch the blood tang of meat.

I have been to Ninfa in autumn when it was clear and bright and spent the whole day with only my wife and been there in spring in the rain when around every corner the roses exceeded themselves and the green of grass, foliage and undergrowth shone like looking at the world through an emerald. It was equally stunning in different ways and Lauro says that he loves it best in autumn, when the bones reveal themselves. I think that the secret of Ninfa, as perhaps with all truly great gardens, is that it enlarges us. Rather than standing on the outside and admiring, as we walk through we are revealed aspects of the physical and spiritual world that belong to us and which, by sharing, we possess. There is a complete lack of arrogance in this, a sense of wonder rather than pride, that is profoundly and enduringly uplifting. When I asked Lauro what his philosophy of care was for Ninfa he smiled and just said, "We are guests upon this earth." And when you are at Ninfa, you are an honoured one.

One last thing. After spending a long day in the garden I stayed a few miles away in the little hilltop town of Sermoneta. Returning to my room after midnight, I opened the windows overlooking the plain where Ninfa's tower could still just be made out. Dogs barked in relay and too many cars chased the roads. But from inside that noise and from within the darkness I could make out the sound of clear, liquid birdsong and for half an hour I stood and listened entranced as the nightingales at Ninfa sang and sang.

Previous pages: Dawn at Ninfa. Spring. The garden spans the river that rises in the hills just above the garden and which flows with water that is as clear as the crystal light of early morning.

Above: The entrance garden with the tower in the background. Water in this section has been channelled and trained to overlap and cross in streams and rivulets all running down to the river. One feature is the way that the mown grass runs right to the water's edge.

Above: Ninfa is made from the ruins of a town abandoned in 1381. The streets and buildings all remain but populated by plants rather than people. Here the yellow flowers of *Caesalpina decapetala* crowd into a lane.

Opposite top: Tightly pollarded willows in the fields abutting the garden. The estate has two thousand acres devoted to preserving the ecology of the surrounding landscape with the same sensitivity that made and conserves the garden.

Opposite bottom: Roses garland the water's edge. Wherever you are at Ninfa, as you wander its lost streets, you are drawn back to the water. It is, for the three hundred metres or so as it passes on and through the garden, hypnotic and magical.

Top: The garden is looked after with scrupulous attention to detail and the lightest of touches. Every care is taken to preserve the sense of naturalness and wonder – and it takes a great deal of care and skill to achieve this.

Bottom: Oranges growing with a thicket of bamboo behind. The winters can be harsh at Ninfa and some of the more tender citrus invariably succumb to the cold.

Opposite: Ninfa is a garden of glimpses. There is no panoramic view or bigger picture, just a series of scenes happened upon at the corner of a building or a bend in the river that are as beautiful and romantic as in any garden in the world.

Above: The Ponte del Macello, crossing the river by the town wall. There is an open square vent over one of its twin arches which was made so that butchers could bring meat up river to the town during times of plague. Baskets would be lowered from the bridge to the boats below, and the meat drawn up through the holes.

Rome

My connection with Torrecchia is tenuous but personal. When I was beginning to make my own garden in Herefordshire in the mid-1990s I rang Pershore College to see if they had any students keen to do part-time work for me. Yes they said. They had just the fellow. Immensely keen, hard-working and a very nice chap to boot. They were right. He turned out to be Stuart Barfoot, then around nineteen and almost as fixated with gardens and gardening as I was. The children and dogs liked him too. It is always a good sign. Stuart moved on from college and I followed his career through the horticultural grapevine, hearing that he was working in Provence, Beirut and Italy. Glamorous stuff – but then he always was a cut above the average horticultural student.

At the same time a young, poetic garden designer was making his name. This was Dan Pearson and I remember filming him as he prepared for his first Chelsea show garden in 1994. From the first it was clear that Dan was a breath of genuinely exciting, albeit very refined and stylish, air into what was a rather staid British gardening establishment.

Two very wealthy Italians had visited Chelsea that year, seen Dan's work and decided that he was exactly the person that they needed to work on their garden. They were Prince Carlo Caracciolo, a newspaper magnate, and his wife Violante, sister of the billionaire industrialist and head of Fiat, Gianni Agnelli.

In 1990 Carlo Caracciolo had bought the 1,500 hectare estate of Torrecchia in Cisterna di Latini, sight unseen, about an hour south of Rome and a few miles north of Ninfa. He did not visit it for months but when he finally did both he and Violante fell in love with it. It is not hard to see why. The house is built in the ruins of a medieval castle and its satellite village, abandoned in the thirteenth century, which in turn is set in an astonishingly beautiful wooded valley. The five-kilometre drive from the road takes you through flower-filled meadows that beggar many a border and this incredible natural beauty sets the tone for the garden.

Carlo and Violante had the former granary converted to a house by the architect Gae Aulenti and asked Lauro Marchetti at Ninfa to make a garden around it and in amongst the ruins. Unlike Ninfa which evolved more or less steadily over a century, the Caracciolos wanted their garden as quickly as possible and were happy to spend what ever it took to attain that. Mature trees were planted, including three 80-year-old oaks. Lauro oversaw the installation of over 10,000 plants over four years but the demands of Ninfa were too great to give sufficient time to Torrecchia. This is when Dan took over the supervisory role and in 1998 he in turn hired a young but widely experienced Englishman to be Head Gardener. This was Stuart Barfoot.

Stuart did not know a word of Italian when he arrived, was naturally reserved and shy and one of the existing two gardeners was under the impression that he was coming as his assistant, which posed all kinds of linguistic and management problems, but he and the garden soon flourished.

I met Stuart – for the first time in fifteen years – and he took me to Torrecchia which is not open to the public. He no longer works there as a gardener but has set up his own design business and acts as consultant to the estate, visiting every month. You arrive at the fortifications of a large castle but no manicured neatness. There is none of the sub-hotel formality that can be the default position for many large houses. Through the gatehouse and in front of the converted granary everything is lush, slightly shaggy and very green. A touch of formality is held in the pomegranates underplanted with dozens of box balls but even they are fuzzy with new growth and unclipped in spring. "Those pomegranates were tiny when I arrived," Stuart told me. But then the hedges he helped plant in my garden are now twenty feet tall. As at Ninfa, the energy between vigorous growth and the slow decay of the buildings is what gives the garden its dynamic and, rather curiously, its harmony.

Although there is the whitest of white gardens with foxgloves, aquilegias, nicotiania, white valerian and an enormous white mock orange flowering simultaneously – which of course they could never do in England – Stuart told me that "The idea is to let as many things as possible look as though they have seeded themselves." So the steps round to the back are smothered with daisies, valerian grows out at angle from the base of the house and a white rose sprawls out halfway across the staircase. Although there is a whole northern European and American school of carefully managed, loose, informal planting it is challenging stuff if you are used to the order and symmetrical balance of most gardens. I asked what Italians made of it. "A lot of people don't get it," Stuart said. "I came here one morning to find a visitor weeding out all the flowers in the cobbles and I had to explain that I resowed them every year."

When Stuart came he encouraged them to let as much grass as possible grow long, just mowing paths where necessary, and his latest addition to the garden is an annual wildflower meadow. When I was there in mid-May it was at its very best, filled with camomile, cornflowers and poppies with a narrow path arching through it. It is strimmed every September and raked up before being rotavated and resown anew each year. "The only slight problem," Stuart said, "is that we have to keep the birds off until the seed has germinated. Other than that it is no work at all."

A tiny stream raced down between mown grass and a border like a furious raingutter and we followed it to the large shell of a building which had a rectangular pool. The ground was speckled with *Allium christophii* and 'Purple Sensation' and mulleins and field poppies grew in the gaping window places framing the view out over the valley with its oak woods and flowery meadows. Instead of a path around the pool was an annual meadow, cut and resown every year. It is an inspired idea. Some seats were shaded by a vast wisteria. Around the walls were half a dozen huge terracotta pots with oranges, the soil of which also sprouted salvias and alliums doing their best to look like weeds. Everything, of course, was deliberate, nurtured and selectively tweaked to make it look as naturally overgrown as possible. There is no irony in this – after all, that is essentially what any gardening is –

fiddling with plants to make them look as you would wish. It may look slightly abandoned and scruffy but it didn't come cheap. Apparently each pot cost 1,300 euros and needed a crane to hoist them in.

Down below is the lake with white water lilies and silver carp burping bubbles at us. It was originally made by Lauro but Dan and Stuart doubled it in size and dammed the water to make cascades and then planted it with iris from Ninfa and great rafts of zantedeschia. The undergrowth reveals a grotto-like arched recess of square water entirely covered with pea-green algae. It is extraordinarily beautiful. "Four metres deep," said Stuart. Beautiful and alarming. The woods come right up to the battlements of the garden and I asked if they had any particular pest problems. "Just wild boar and porcupine."

It seems that the key to this garden is its relationship to the estate around it. Indeed I am sure that everyone connected to it would agree that nothing inside the walls is more beautiful than the landscape seen looking out from the garden. The great success is the harmony between those two landscapes, the tightly domestic and the broadly managed. There are obvious links – the fencing and stakes are from the chestnut woods, the cyclamen that flower in the grass in the autumn are all taken from the estate as are the narcissi that replace them in spring as well as the matteuccia fern that grows freely all over the shaded corners of the garden. But it is subtler than that. Despite – perhaps because of – the enormous walls and centuries of history, the landscape has grown into the garden and the garden has welcomed it and gone out to meet it half way. It shows what inspired patrons and brilliant young gardeners can do between them. The only irony is that the latter are British working in an Italian garden rather than Italians. Whilst I feel a flush of associated pride at seeing Stuart's work, I also feel that it is a real regret that modern Italy values the skills of gardening so little. Its long and glorious garden history needs to be upheld not just by money and good taste but by intelligent, educated gardeners in love with the earth that they work.

Opposite: Wisteria drapes an arch of the abandoned castle of Torrecchia. The garden is planted and carefully tended to create the impression that everything is growing as naturally and spontaneously as possible to preserve the atmosphere suggested by the castle ruins. This takes a huge amount of skill and management.

Above: The flower meadow rich with camomile, cornflowers, daisies and poppies in early May. This is resown annually in September after being cut, raked up and rotavated. The seed mix is specially chosen and adjusted to suit the soil, desired flowering season and location.

Rome

Of course Hadrian's Villa is not really a garden as we would acknowledge it any more than the Forum in Rome or Hadrian's Wall in Northumberland are gardens. But it did include many different gardens and – really importantly – was a big influence on the makers of the great sixteenth-century gardens.

To set the scene. Until the fifteenth century the classical world was largely forgotten or ignored. The Church saw the studying or depiction of any religion or gods other than Christianity as blasphemy. The great development of the Renaissance, first through the study and dissemination of classical texts and then through sculpture and architecture, was the discovery of the classical Roman and Greek world. It was a dramatic transformation from the medieval, Gothic mindset to one that embraced and used classical forms, ideas and concepts as part of a modern way of expressing and interpreting the world.

A hundred years after this movement began in literature and art and arguably at the very end of the Renaissance, the classical influences appeared as an integral part of garden design. Castello and the Boboli Gardens in Florence, Villa d'Este just down the road from Hadrian's Palace (to call it a villa is useful shorthand but bears no relation to the site which is enormous – bigger than the whole of Pompeii), Villa Lante, Villa Farnese and dozens more all returned to classical antiquity to adorn and illustrate their gardens.

In many cases this was literal as thousands of sculptures and stones were taken from their original sites and installed in the gardens of the powerful, and this was a process of pilfering that went on right through to the twentieth century – not least by visiting British aristocracy in the eighteenth and nineteenth centuries.

But equally important was the study and inspiration both of sites and specific works. From the early sixteenth until the twentieth century, gardens became dominated by classical statuary, buildings and water and nowhere was more influential in this than Hadrian's Villa in Tivoli. Palladio, Michelangelo, Leonardo and Ligorio all studied it and Ligorio was the first to survey it and also excavated parts of it before starting his work on Villa d'Este.

Hadrian ruled as emperor of the Roman Empire for twenty-one years from 117AD to 138AD and his villa is a palace for the most powerful man in the world with wealth that beggars modern imagination. That power sowed a seed. Renaissance princes and cardinals could gaze on these ruins and get a hint of the secret of true material power. To emulate the physical appearance of it might conjure the absolute expression of it.

Perhaps. Perhaps it just struck the right note for that particular, extraordinary period and place in history.

But much of their attention was focused on one part of the Villa which was the Canopus. This is now a long pool flanked by banks topped by stone pines with a few restored columns and arches at one end and the ruins of the nymphaeum at the other. The water is a rich green with the pines reflecting as a splash of deeper green within it. Half a dozen white caryatids hint at what was there two thousand years ago. It is both astonishingly impressive and beautiful and, through lack of money and perhaps will, there is a tantalising amount still to be excavated.

In Hadrian's time it would have been a colonnaded stretch of water with statues all the way round, culminating in the large building with its great arched and domed opening covering a semi-circular eating area and stretching back to a raised nave-like hall, the whole thing performing as a banqueting house. The guests lay in an inclined stone semi-circle, thrillingly close to the emperor himself who ate in the recessed platform set above them. Water was everywhere. There were two large basins before and behind Hadrian, open to the sky so the sun bounced off the surface and spangled out again onto the white marble walls. Water ran down the walls of the semi-circle into a canal behind the guests and from a fountain in the middle of them and out into the pool in front of them. Water provided music, movement and coolness in the unbearable heat of summer. Water has symbolism and meaning that could be read and admired. The garden pulsed to the rhythm of water rather than the modern beat of plants.

The pool may have represented the canal at the Egyptian town of Canopus or the Mediterranean. The nymphaeum is modelled on the temple of Serapis. The point of this is not exactly what is represented but that the buildings, water and statues all had meaning. From the 1550s and especially Ligorio's excavations onwards, it became apparent that the language of the Canopus and of classical allusion could be incorporated into gardens both to increase their aesthetic appeal and to tell the stories that you wanted the visitor to hear.

All there are to see now are beautiful ruins. But they remain substantially the same or even better than those that Ligorio and his contemporaries were so inspired by. To understand any of the gardens of Italy made in the sixteenth century – and arguably in Europe for centuries thereafter – you have to visit Hadrian's Palace and the Canopus. This is where those gardens came from.

Above and opposite: The Canopus of Hadrian's Villa at Tivoli. This long rectangular pool, originally arcaded all round by caryatids and columns, was a huge influence on High Renaissance gardens. The villa was visited by every great artist and architect of the age, including Leonardo da Vinci, Michelangelo and Ligorio (who surveyed the site and used it, metaphorically and physically, stealing cartloads of stone and statues, for Villa d'Este a couple of miles up the hill). The pool culminated in a huge domed banqueting house lined in white marble. Water ran down the walls into a semi-circular canal around which the guests lay with Hadrian seated high above them, God-like, in a marble bay. The combination of balance and harmony, the engineering ingenuity that made water move and the idea of a garden as a spectacle and entertainment was the key to the great Italian gardens of the late sixteenth and early seventeenth centuries.

Rome

No garden exemplifies the High Renaissance ability to transform a landscape and make it dance and sing to order like Villa d'Este. Garden making on a grand scale reached a kind of apogee in Italy in the middle of the sixteenth century and Villa d'Este is the grandest of them all.

Of all the wealthy, ambitious pack of prelates circling the sixteenth-century papacy, Cardinal Ippolito d'Este was the richest. His family, based in Ferrara, accrued enormous wealth from their control of the best cannon-making techniques in Europe. Ippolito d'Este grew up not only rich but also steered towards power. He was made a bishop at the age of two, Archbishop of Milan at ten as well as receiving a long list of benefices that provided him with much of his wealth, although he was not ordained a priest until the age of fifty-five in 1564, six years before his death. In 1549, at the age of forty, he returned to Rome after thirteen years in France spent as Ambassador of Ferrara to the court of Francis I and on the death of Alessandro Farnese, Pope Paul III, in November of that year, eyed the papacy covetously. However, after ten weeks of intense political wrangling that involved d'Este playing a major role in blocking the claims of Alessandro Farnese of Caprarola, the conclave elected Cardinal Del Monte who took the name of Julius III. Julius III rewarded d'Este with the governorship of Tivoli, some twenty miles east of Rome and spent the rest of his life making it his summer residence creating one of the most spectacular gardens of his or any age.

The cardinal's choice of architect was Pirro Ligorio and Villa d'Este his enduring masterpiece. He had been Superintendent to Ancient Monuments in Rome and in 1549 began excavations of Hadrian's Villa a mile or two down the hill from the site of Villa d'Este and plundered statues and stone as well as taking inspiration.

Before the garden could begin the site had to be prepared. Whole streets of the town of Tivoli were swept away in the steep valley below the monastic buildings which became d'Este's villa. Nature was tamed and bought to a suitable state of submission in order that a very controlled beauty could be imposed onto it. This clearing took up much of the first few years of work and in 1555, after the death of Julius II, the governorship of Tivoli was taken from him and he was banished to his home town of Ferrara. Work on the Villa d'Este was suspended for four years until Pope Pius IV died and he was reinstated as governor of Tivoli and work could continue until his death in 1572.

The modern visitor enters the garden from the monastery, which means that you start with the extraordinary view north across the tops of the trees and perfectly squared tiers of hedges, but the garden is designed to be entered from the bottom and the old road from Rome and it is worth heading straight down, barely looking left or right, in order to slowly follow the narrative of the garden as intended as you make your way back up the steep hill.

The design is superficially simple with a central path taking you straight up via a series of fountains and steep steps with terraces diverting you on either side with various displays, statues and attractions like a kind of horticultural fairground made of stone. Diagonal flights of steps crisscross and interconnect the steeper terraces until you finally arrive at the doorway out of the villa to look back and survey the wonder of all you have walked through.

Illustrations show that originally the lower garden had a covered walkway leading to the fishponds with mazes set on either side and today this area feels slightly incomplete and park-like in comparison to the higher levels. But there is much restoration work taking place and perhaps it will eventually be done. However, once you reach the fishponds then the wonders start to pile upon each other. There are three rectangular fishponds in series across the width of the garden and, although a fourth was intended, it was never built. They are lovely in themselves as well being a practical necessity to maintain the Cardinal's household in fresh fish. One end opens out over the landscape falling below but the other end dominates everything else. This is The Fountain of the Organ. Standing in front of it is like standing in a city square before a colossal church. The extravagance of money, space, stone, water and skill is so extreme that it is hard to take in but the more gardens I visit and each time I go back to Villa d'Este the more this is impressed on me. It is princely and palatial in its scope.

The Organ Fountain was designed by Luc Leclerc, the French assistant to Maccarone, and the power of the water forces air through pipes to play tunes. Interestingly piped music in all its modern forms has robbed it of any power to astonish yet in its day it must have seemed little short of miraculous.

The first steps (of many) rise ahead with cascades running down the banisters to the next terrace with The Fountain of the Dragons and curved stairs sweeping round it up to the next level. The four dragons lean back spreading their leathery wings and baring their fat bellies whilst they spout water. It is yet another expression of power: see, they seem to say, even we, fire-breathing monsters that we are, are tamed to perform exactly how and where our master bids.

We are used to city gardens making pools and oases of countryside in the town but Villa d'Este repeatedly brings the town into the garden with its fountains, steps and paths like streets and separate sections built up to be piazzas. Flowers and flowerbeds – and there are some in the garden where the irises were looking particularly good on my last Maytime visit – are incidental. The garden strives to encompass every manifestation of civilisation as envisaged by a well-educated, wealthy cardinal aching for power in 1560. It narrows the field down to something almost imaginable if not achievable.

The Fountain of the Owl with its hidden sprays and moving, singing birds, Rometta with its boat on a miniature Tiber and little Romescape are both more Portmeirion than Sissinghurst. The symbolism was plain – encompassing Rome (and thus the power of the papacy) in his garden and it was apparently much used for performances and masques. For all its finish and grandeur, this adds a kind of period charm that is utterly unmodern.

But connecting Rometta and The Oval or Tivoli Fountain (which was under scaffolding on my last visit) is the wonder of the garden, a piece of genius outside and above any period constraints. This is The Hundred Fountains which I regard as one of the most beautiful features of any garden anywhere in the world. It is one of those pieces of work that enlarges and improves everyone who sees it.

Its power lies in the simple repetition that builds to an enormous orchestral effect. Each of the water jets is small with a top tier spouting up, a middle tier falling down the wallface into a long narrow basin and emerging through the mouths of gargoyles to spout into a stone-edged, waist-high canal. This runs for over 130 metres along the entire length of the terrace linking The Tivoli Fountain to Rometta and, as you stroll along, it grows into something more than the sum of its parts. It is – and there is no point in being coy about this – a profound work of art worth a trip from anywhere else to see.

There is a kind of aesthetic irony in that it would neither have looked nor was intended to have looked as it does now when it was made. All along the back of the facade are reliefs showing scenes from Ovid's *Metamorphoses*, now limed-up and faded to the point of indecipherability. The fleur-de-lys and eagles – both d'Este symbols – were added later in 1622 and the obelisks in 1685. The whole thing would have had the garish crispness of the newly restored Owl Fountain rather than the lovely green softness that we now see. It would have not been so nice.

But I like the crisp, theme-park sharpness of the current restorations. This is how it was meant to be in 1572 when d'Este died and the garden was almost finished. It was a world where money bought you colour and sharp edges, and taste ran easily from Palestrina masses and Michelangelo to brash water fountains and lurid colours. It would be challenging to see The Hundred Fountains restored from their current combination of muzzy fern and soft stone with crystalline water to their 1622 condition, shocking even, but hardly wrong. The one inconsistency in the garden are the trees that have been allowed to grow enormously tall. They are, to the modern eye, lovely things but historically absurd.

Above and overleaf: There are over fifty different fountains in Villa d'Este but this, The Fountain of the Organ, is the biggest and most dramatic. The garden was begun in 1550 and from the outset was intended to impress. It necessitated moving streets, diverting the local river and has been estimated to cost over a hundred million euros at modern values. No part is more obviously impressive than this enormous fountain with the roar and spray of water. The organ plays by water forcing air through its pipes and was considered a wonder in its day although now, in this age of piped music, it seems tame against the sheer scale of the display.

Opposite: The modern entrance to the garden is through the villa at the top but visitors were intended to approach from the bottom and work their way up the hillside, climbing many flights of stairs, overcome with wonder and exhaustion as they got closer to the villa itself. There is a stone trough built into the retaining wall, either side of every step, and water flowed from one to another descending with a gentle gurgle – deliciously cool in the baking summer heat.

Above: The statue of Diana of Ephesus, the pre-Hellenic Goddess of fertility, spouts water from her many breasts. Copied from the original in the Farnese collection in Rome, she was part of The Fountain of the Organ, but was moved to a site in the lower garden in 1611.

Opposite: The simple repetition of the modest spouts and jets builds up to a majestic orchestral effect as you walk the 130 metres of The Hundred Fountains lining the entire width of the garden. It originally took five years to make and all along the back of the facade are reliefs showing scenes from Ovid's

Metamorphoses now limed-up and faded to the point of indecipherability. The whole thing – like everything in the garden – would have a garish crispness rather than the lovely green softness of the maidenhair ferns and faded stone that we now see.

Overleaf: One of the three fishponds in the centre of the garden. A mock medieval tower looks out over the landscape below. In a garden filled with sound and fury, this is the still, calm centre. It was also an important source of fish for the Cardinal's table.

Rome

A building could scarcely dominate a town more than Villa Aldobrandini hunkers over Frascati. It looks enormous and the town huddles at its gates like the offices and quarters of a great estate. This, of course, is deliberate enough although the villa was not built until the end of the sixteenth century, by which time Frascati was ancient. It is another Renaissance monied interloper, swaggering in with money and friends in high places and the arrogance of power, and hurrah – at least from the distance of four centuries – for that. But for all its magnificence, anyone visiting the Aldobrandinis and their summer seat in Frascati could only approach as a supplicant, making an ever-steeper haul up the slope to the villa's entrance.

But there is a practical reason for its imposing position above the rest of the town. Water is the key. The Aldobrandinis did – and still do – own and control the water supply to the town and this water was first made to jump through its horticultural hoops before passing on and down to sustain those below. He who controls water controls almost everything. Frascati was the preferred summer seat of the Renaissance cardinals vying for precedence and there was literally not enough water to go round. By cornering the market Aldobrandini trumped them all.

I arrived in the centre of Frascati on a spectacularly vile spring morning and the villa was merely a misty outline through the rain. Water everywhere and most of it seeping through my pathetically inadequate waterproofs.

Despite the wet, a tractor was flailing the grass on the steep slope either side of the wonderful hedged approach up the hill beyond the main gates. From a distance this looks like a hedge with a mazy rivulet of a path running through it but it is in fact an overgrown line of holm oaks whose exterior has been clipped to a monstrous hedge but the interior is made up of a cloistered strip of woodland vaulted with large, branchy oaks. It is worth coming just for this alone. I was later told by Prince Aldobrandini that his grandmother created this vast hedge-walk by cutting down the two woods flanking the original central approach, leaving just the trees along the very edge that grew together to create a tunnel.

Villa Aldobrandini has none of the shiny glamour of Villa d'Este or Villa Lante. It is not so much that it is uncared for – evidence of work is there at every turn – but despite its enormous size and evident grandeur, it has a frank aura of benign neglect. Now I like this. I like the moss on the coping between the terracotta pots with the clipped box but like even more that there are forty such huge pots, each accumulating beauty on each other. I like the huge, empty niches ready to juggle water in its carved stone reaches. The grandeur is careless and unselfconscious, far from the shiny, clean authenticity of d'Este and in its shabbiness much more appealing to the modern eye.

This is the key to the garden. It is not a museum. Hardly anyone comes and those that do take much of it for granted. The old servants' quarters are leased to the Financial Police as their headquarters and a mixture of squad cars, joggers and dog walkers passed through the middle of the garden without a sideways glance. The Aldobrandini family still owns the villa and lives there, amongst other homes. So nothing has to please a paying public. This is a rare thing amongst the great Italian houses and gives Aldobrandini a unique character amongst a tranche of great Renaissance gardens that all share the same small world of papal and political intrigue from the same period. It has something of the air of a country estate, with fields, vineyards, kiwi plantations and a tractor parked next to the stylishly scruffy cars by the front door, yet Frascati is a heaving suburb of Rome which laps up in urban waves against the gates. This takes much of the strain away from the garden. Nothing is asked of it beyond that which it carelessly gives away.

The land in front of the house are grounds. The gardens are hidden and private and once round behind the building the whole tenor and tone changes. It is enchanting. Whereas the front facade is a block of power, the back of the building is elegant and charming and faces a curving wall filled with niches, fountains and statues. This is The Water Theatre and one of the great dramatic setpieces of all gardens anywhere in the world. You step into something like a stable yard with a vast ballroom attached.

It is apparently a faded shadow of its original self which, when it was completed, was an all-singing, all-dancing, watery production with jets spouting from orifices and nozzles at every turn, playing tunes, spraying unsuspecting visitors and fulfilling all the aspirational fantasies of the papal jet set intent upon impressing one another with their gardens. A glimpse at the extraordinarily ornate dining room or Temple to Apollo gives a hint at the rollicking ornateness of house and gardens. What remains is a bleached-out, beautiful ghost. I think of these cardinals vying for papal affection and power like courtiers of Elizabeth I spending fortunes on rebuilding their houses in the hope that the queen would favour them with a visit on her endless peregrinations.

Now the statues that originally lined the balustrade have gone. Napoleon (whose sister married a Borghese) took all the statues from the niches saying that he would repay them when he returned from Russia but, as Prince Aldobrandini told me with a wry smile, "Events got in the way…" The central globe held by The Atlas Organ plays no more tunes and the flutes that the muses played have disappeared. Estate workers saunter across to lunch. A small dog stops, barks once and prances on its way. Rusty scaffolding meshes one side of the flanking buildings. Washing hangs from a window set above a colonnaded arch. But what is left still remains overwhelmingly impressive and made all the more dramatic for its slightly domestic setting.

Either side of the villa there are matching gardens dominated by wonderfully scarred plane trees, all planted in the 1850s but looking much older than the buildings and terracing that are twice their age. A collection of hydrangeas is under-planted on the one side and the other butts up against the Financial Police. These trees are a lovely sculpture but are, apparently, dying. May their death be long and slow. My first visit was in early May when the hydrangeas were leafy but subdued. However, when I dropped in again in mid-July they had doubled in size and frothed shamelessly around the base of each plane like pompomed, pastel tutus as shamelessly larky as a wonderful drag act.

To the right of the villa a series of box-hedged gardens unfolds but half-used, half-forgotten as though a plan was made but then lost. From what was the kitchen garden a Chilean pine grows butting onto a ginko, the remnants of a passing collecting fad. It is like rummaging through an attic, opening doors into rooms whose use has long been forgotten. A vast stone basin collects leaves. I love this, love the loss and survival, the way that gardens slip away into a kind of reverie. But the real fabric is before and aft of the villa and these remnants are literally sideshows to The Musical Theatre.

The theatre itself is the culmination of the performance that began high up above it. From the ground you can see a cascade stepping down to the balustrade with a tall pair of columns flanking it. Either side of them is an astonishing clipped holm oak hedge, as tall as a house. We groundlings crane up, applaud and take breathless pictures from every angle. But the design is not really for us. The key viewing position is from a loggia set on the fourth floor of the villa where Pietro Aldobrandini and his most privileged guests – who occasionally included his uncle Pope Clement VIII – would gather. Once settled they would look across directly at the colonnades and appreciate the water spiralling down them into the balustrades either side of the cascade, each step of which was an individual pool.

There was more. The visitor now climbs up past the cascade to an area of recently cleared woodland and evident garden archaeology which is hardly more than a tantalising glimpse of the original garden which was bombed to bits in the Second World War. Prints show it to start with a rustic fountain (that has been largely restored by Prince Camillo) falling in from woodland and rough stone with crystal clarity, taking wild nature and channelling her into a courtly masque through various water steps, theatres, fountains and tropes to what still survives. This is fancy now of course. The place is a gnarled Gothic tangle of memory and archeology. You squidge through mud and undergrowth to find these things. But they are there, half hidden, like the screaming mouth carved into the rock, which must surely be a direct lift from Bomarzo. Restoration is underway. It could all be made entire again. But in doing so something would surely be lost.

Villa Aldobrandini stands above the
main square in Frascati, dominating
the town. The clipped holm oaks
flanking the wonderful crazed path
leading up from the main gates are
the only surviving trees from the wood
that originally stood in front of the villa.

Clipped box in terracotta pots beat a
stately rhythm along the retaining walls
of the terraces in front of the house.
The view is towards Rome, keeping an
eye on the seat of papal power.

Overleaf: The scale of Villa Aldobrandini,
with its walls of rendered stone and
clipped oak, as monumental as each
other, is designed to impress as you
approach from town. But it has an
aristocratic insouciance, which means
its grandness is weathered so that it has
become as faded and soft as a tapestry.

Opposite: The wonderfully twisted and gnarled plane trees planted in the middle of the nineteenth century are underplanted with hydrangeas with The Water Theatre and its enormous holm oak hedge above it in the background.

Above: The Water Theatre behind the house is one of the great icons of baroque gardens. The water, bought in by a specially built five-kilometre long aqueduct, comes down from a series of fountains and canals above (all bombed in the Second World War) before tumbling down a cascade and appearing from the central fountain of Atlas holding the globe as well as spouts and jets around the theatre. The statues 'played' flutes and organs powered by the water. Hidden jets would spurt sprays of water to catch unwary guests if they wandered closer. It was not so much water theatre as water Grand Opera.

Rome

"You're not going there, are you?" Claudia said, aghast. "You know the story, don't you?" "It's the British Embassy," I said. "No, it was the Gestapo headquarters in the war. It is a torture building! It is a horrible place."

Some of this is true. Villa Wolkonsky, just by San Giovanni di Laterano, northeast of the Colosseum, is the British Embassy in Rome – sort of, although it is properly the residence of the ambassador with the chancery, the office, a kilometre away in Porta Pia. It was the German Embassy from 1922 until they retreated from Rome in 1944, the Gestapo headquarters were nearby and they may well have had prisons in the basement. Gestapo plus prison tended to also mean torture. But that particular horror does not walk the garden. It is too old for one thing. There are enough layers of history for that particular example of man's inhumanity to man to soak too deep.

Any planting hole in central Rome will become an archaeological dig if you go deep enough but not every garden has thirty-six bays of a full-blown aqueduct in its garden, each bay as big as a tall bridge and the whole thing amounting to a vast garden wall almost two thousand years old. What we see, I was told by the Ambassador's wife, Nicola Chaplin, is merely the top section as a third of it, like most of ancient Rome, is submerged beneath fathoms of soil. She also told me that from high up on one of the embassy buildings you can look down onto the top of the aqueduct and see how precise and controlled is the channelling for the water, how exquisitely exact the engineering.

Once past the sunglassed troops carrying machine guns like fashion accessories and through the inevitable tight security, you are in a curiously unreal world of carefully cultivated normality that is in almost every respect highly abnormal. This part of Rome was open countryside till the seventeenth century and as late as 1830 was vineyards and vegetable gardens. It became a garden after 1830 when Princess Wolkonsky, wife of Prince Nikita Wolkonsky who was an aide-de-camp to Tsar Alexander I, bought the site, made a modest villa in three bays of the aqueduct and laid out a garden around it. She planted roses everywhere and adorned the site with the plaques, busts, sculptures and fragments of stone that every excavation revealed. Apparently she never lived there but used it almost as a country retreat from her apartment by The Tivoli Fountain. After her death a large chunk of the land was sold off and at the end of the nineteenth century a new house was built. The gardens remained noteworthy and Baedeker of 1904 points out that they could be visited on Tuesday and Saturday mornings. After the First World War the villa was sold to the German government who increased its size and used it as their embassy. A swimming pool was added to the garden which was by all accounts maintained well. During the war the Gestapo had their headquarters nearby but might have used the cellars – with their steel doors, grills and spyholes – as prisons and torture chambers.

The Germans left Villa Wolkonsky in 1944 and in 1947 the British Embassy took up temporary home there after their own was blown up by Zionists. In 1951 the British bought it and it has been the British Ambassador's residence ever since although in 1971, when the old embassy was rebuilt, the embassy offices moved back to Porta Pia. This means that Villa Wolkonsky has a slightly ambivalent role as private home and very busy, rather public face of the Embassy.

I arrived at 8.30A.M. on a Saturday morning (Baedeker would have approved) and wandered round whilst delegations arrived containing officials and guests in their best clothes and on their best behaviour. Drivers in ties and jeans smoked in a huddle outside. Rome is everywhere in the garden. In the air from the traffic outside, through the trees that almost surround it (and almost hide the razor wire looped along the garden wall), in every nook and cranny in the shape of Princess Wolkonsky's artefacts, in the form and shadow of the aqueduct and in the palpable sense of yards of solid history beneath your feet. Yet there is something very British about it too, with its vegetable plot with rows of cabbages and cut flowers shaded by a large olive tree. I cannot imagine any Italian garden that is so self-consciously public, showing its vegetable plot in this way.

The garden is long and narrow, tapering to a triangle, and a central gravel path, flanked by immaculately clipped yew hedges, runs down the centre, parallel to the aqueduct. Lavender softens its edges. Stone pines, with trunks clean to fifty feet or more, tower above. The stone pines of Rome are the most impressive and elegant of all city trees. Put one or two on a patch of grass and you have a beautiful garden. The path leads down to a round temple assembled from five columns and a conical roof containing the most perfect sculpture I have seen in any garden, anywhere. It is an armless marble torso of Venus donated by a former ambassador, Sir Ashley Clark. To encounter it, lit from the surrounding dark by a shaft of morning sun, was a frozen moment of pure beauty.

There are beehives behind the temple for ambassadorial honey and marmalade is made from the ambassadorial oranges of which there are plenty, although all were a gleaming green when I was there. Despite the relatively recent provenance of vineyards and vegetable plots on the site, this mixture of the home-made and home-grown has a touch of hearty, best-foot-forward home sickness about it. To confuse things more it is a longing for a home that lingers truer in the grander embassies than back home.

Either side of the central path, running between the boundary on one side and the visual barrier of the aqueduct on the other, are a series of conventional, very English rooms with lawns, Lutyens seats and lots of roses, yet the palms, pomegranates, bougainvilleas, brugmansias, Olearias and citrus testify to the baking heat of Roman summers and mildness of the winter. A silk tree, *Albizia julibriissin*, too tender to survive for long anywhere in Britain, is festooned with flat pods that follow on from the mass of apricot-coloured flowers. Through one of the arches of the aqueduct I see a pet cemetery: 'Myrtle the Turtle 1991–2000' lies next to 'Champers' and 'Camilla 1982–98'. A basin, made under a closed-in arch and adorned with knobbly limestone as a token grotto, has a crocodile head peaking over the lip. I half-expect to see a child's bike flung down or a football in a border. These things, amongst all the archeology, are curiously moving. But the villa and its surrounding grand hedges of bay and striped lawns are the equivalent of a horticultural stiff upper lip. What remains is a reminder, amongst the very Italian outward show of astonishing ruins, sculpture and beautifully maintained gardens (by an Australian head gardener – not, of course, an Italian) that whilst the British admire these things hugely, what they love in a garden is its intimacy.

Above: Clipped yew hedges repeat the pattern of the arches of the aqueduct running through the centre of Villa Wolkonsky. The garden is filled with statues, plinths, tablets and archeology excavated during the course of making the garden in the nineteenth century.

Opposite top: The garden is the home of the British Ambassador in Rome and has a British air to it. There are a series of very English rooms with lawns, Lutyens seats and lots of roses, yet the palms, pomegranates, bougainvilleas and citrus testify to the very Roman climate.

Opposite bottom: There are thirty-six bays of the first-century aqueduct in the garden, each bay as big as a tall bridge and the whole thing amounting to a vast garden wall almost two thousand years old. A third of it – along with endless archeology – remains buried.

Viterbo

To the traveller looking at a modern map of Italy, Viterbo is hardly recognisable as a self-contained area at all but in gardening terms it has a real and significant identity of its own. There is an extraordinary quartet of gardens within half an hour's drive of the town. This is not coincidence. All are connected by family, history and location.

It has a dramatic landscape dominated by wooded hills full of ravines with a rough-edged intensity that smoulders rather than rages. It is powerful and primitive and dramatically different to Rome to the south or Tuscany to the north. You will drive through mile upon mile of beech, oak and chestnut woods, the latter grown for their nuts rather than for the long coppiced poles as in Amalfi, and through plantations of hazel in neat blocks, also grown for the nuts and subsequent oil. The Lago di Vico at the base of Mount Cimini and the much bigger Lago di Bolsena, north of Viterbo, are surrounded by woods and there is a distinct sensation that you arrive at everything through a filter of trees.

Viterbo was founded by the Etruscans, and although the centre of Rome is just an hour down the motorway, it remains a very separate place with its lakes and mysterious woods and almost truculent lack of sophistication. But the food is very good, the people warm and walking the summer streets at dusk, half-drunk from the richness of the gardens and perhaps a good bottle of wine, it is a good place to be.

In the thirteenth century, until the papacy removed itself to Avignon for seventy years, it was the home of the popes and the famous papal enclave of 1268–71, which lasted for thirty-three months before the election of Gregory X, was held here. The townspeople had to house and feed them and in the end they blockaded the door, removed the roof and only sent in bread and water. This concentrated their minds wonderfully and a decision soon followed and gave rise to the tradition of the cardinals being holed up in a conclave until a new pope is elected.

For the lover of gardens Viterbo is the perfect place to base yourself when you visit Villa Lante a few miles down the road at Bagnaia, Bomarzo twenty minutes to the west, Castello Ruspoli at Vignanello on

The giant moss-covered figure of Demeter balancing a flower urn on her head in the sacred wood at Bomarzo. Just glimpsed on her left shoulder is a child clambering over her. Like all the sculptures in the garden, she has been carved in situ from a huge natural boulder.

the winding road through chestnut groves to the south and the vast Villa Farnese at Caprarola just ten kilometres or so from Vignanello. All these gardens are entwined by more than geography. Alessandro Farnese who made Caprarola was related by marriage to Vicino Orsini of Bomarzo whose daughter Ottavia made the great parterre at Ruspoli. Cardinal Gambara who made the garden at Villa Lante at Bagnaia was a great friend of Vicino Orsini (as well as Ippolito d'Este at Tivoli) and was related to the Farneses via Beatrice Farnese, Countess of Vignanello. It was a small, enormously wealthy and privileged world.

But a world which in the fifty years between 1552 when Orsini began Bomarzo and 1603 when his daughter Ottavia started the garden at Vignanello produced four of the world's greatest gardens, all made in the heart of the Etruscan countryside, all of which still endure to this day, albeit with some restoration, and all of which can be visited and seen in virtually their original condition.

The key to these gardens is that they were made at a point in history when the western world, and Italy in particular, was reinventing itself. The Protestant movement in northern Europe and the terrible upheavals in Florence and Rome at the beginning of the century had galvanised the Catholic Church into action. These gardens, even Bomarzo in all its oddness, were not passive. Gardens of the Renaissance were seen as places to walk, think and sit and discuss platonic ideals. But by 1550 gardens became much more proactive. They *did* things. They were made in sites that were inhospitable and difficult and had to be tamed, they moved water in vast quantities by astonishingly sophisticated hydro-engineering, and having done that they made every kind of fountain, waterfall and aquatic display. They built sweeping steps and terraces and moved classical statues to adorn the gardens. They were a performance to be admired in their own right rather than a just a backdrop. They were intended, from the outset, to surprise and amaze you and still do.

The water chain at Villa Lante in Bagnaia, the most perfect of all High Renaissance gardens. The water comes from the Dolphin Fountain above and makes its way down the centre of the steps in a series of swirling stone arabesques made liquid by the movement of the water.

Above: You walk up from the Summer garden abutting the Villa, through the Bosco where Cardinal Alessandro Farnese hunted birds and suddenly the Barchetto and its Casino appear through the trees. It is an extraordinarily sophisticated fantasy in the middle of the woods. It was made in 1573, ten years after the lower gardens, expressly as a place for al fresco dining and the Casino was added in 1586 as the cardinal was ageing and needed a roof over his head as he dined. The walls flanking the water chain and the two pavilions at the base were added in the 1620s long after Farnese's death.

Opposite: Manipulating water was considered the highest of arts within the gardens of the High Renaissance. It was channelled into torrents, fountains, elaborate jokes and tricks and spouted from the mouths of incidental sculpture like this face on the wall flanking the curving steps at the Fountain of the Vase.

Overleaf: The fountain of the Vase. Two River Gods flank an enormous vase from which water overflowed. The symbolism would have been clear to Farnese's contemporaries: he was so powerful he could channel the might of a river into a cup and let it spill exactly where he willed.

Previous pages: The great parterre at Villa Lante with the town of Bagnaia butting against the boundary hedge. The complicate broderie pattern in box and yew replaced the original layout in the seventeenth century. The water that runs and plays down through the garden is finally still in the four central pools.

Above: Looking back up from one of the pools in the parterre. The relatively modest casino on the right was built by Cardinal Gambara as his summer residence. In 1598, instead of enlarging it his successor, Cardinal Monalto, built its twin, just glimpsed behind the fountain, balancing the garden.

Opposite top: Lante is full of the noise of water as it makes its way through the garden, here spilling from the water chain (see page 79) over the terrace into the Fountain of the River Gods. The flow is channelled by a giant crayfish – a gambero – the symbol of Cardinal Gambara.

Opposite bottom: One of the wonders of Villa Lante is the enormous stone dining table eighteen metres long with a rill running down its centre through which the water continues to the lower terrace. Dishes would have floated on the water, keeping cool in the icy water.

Opposite: One of the two reclining
River Gods, either Tiber or Arno,
holding a cornucopia in his left hand
and looking supremely relaxed about it.
These enormous figures are similar to
ones at the gardens of Bomarzo and
Caprarola and were obviously familiar
and recognisable symbols of abundance.

Above: The tall columns once supported
an elaborate aviary. Throughout the
sixteenth and seventeenth centuries
aviaries were considered an important
element of a great garden. They were
often built on a magnificent scale and
a good example still exists at Isola Bella
on Lake Maggiore.

To appreciate the Sacro Bosco (Sacred Wood) in Bomarzo you must ruffle your feathers a little and jumble your well-researched Renaissance garden history so it falls awry.

To set the scene. In 1552 Pier Francesco Orsini, the Duke of Orsino, began to make a garden in the woods about a mile below his castle in Bomarzo. As such this was not such an exceptional thing to do. Villa Lante is just a few miles down the road and its maker Cardinal Gambara was a lifelong friend. Orsini was born in 1523, son of Gian Corrado Orsini who inherited the land and left it to his son – widely known as Vicino – when he died in 1535. Vicino was only twelve years old and his elder brother Girolamo was appointed to be his guardian and co-inheritor on the condition that he entered the church. He declined this part of the deal and a raft of other family members pressed their claims to inherit his now abandoned stake in the family estates. The inheritance went to arbitration by the Vice Chancellor of the Papal Estates, Cardinal Alessandro Farnese. The title is grand but it belonged to a boy just three years older than Vicino who went on to make his own extraordinary garden in Caprarola just thirty kilometres or so south of Bomarzo.

The Orsini were one of the great Italian families with three popes to their credit but in the mid-sixteenth century they wielded much less influence than the Farneses and this inevitably meant that they had much less money. Vicino married into the Farnese family and their money helped to make the Sacro Bosco yet it is evident from correspondence that Vicino always felt beholden. However he was a much-admired soldier (often under the command of the Farnese), poet and aesthete. He seems to have been, in an age dominated by bankers and scheming clerics, a man of admirably direct action and appetite.

In describing the man every commentator struggles to put context and shape on his garden. But it resists explanation and it is telling that it only came to modern prominence after Salvador Dalí paid it a visit in 1949 and subsequently championed it. The confusing juxtaposition of the familiar in a strange context along with the fantastic in an ordinary setting made the Sacro Bosco a perfect icon for surrealism. It is shadowed by riddles, puns, emblems and ironies, and straining to understand them misses the point.

Work on the garden began in 1552 and continued until Orsini died in 1584. Although Orsini was away much during this period and work will have started and stopped, it was clearly much more than a passing game or stony masque in the wood. It is an expensive, sustained and elaborate work played out to complex rules that we can only guess at and every visitor makes them up anew. Trying to decode it translates poetry into prose and robs it of its magic and mystery. It is a dream. Nothing is real.

The wood has been cut down at least once and photographs exist of the statues standing in a barren landscape, looking shorn. The modern trees are immature and insubstantial all much, much younger than the garden. But all the substance is in the sculptures. After Orsini's death the Sacro Bosco seems to have been ignored until restoration work began in 1954 by the Bettini family. It was exorcised by a local bishop in 1980 and then, duly defused, opened to the public.

The garden stands on its own. There is no drifting out through windows or views from a building. You and every visitor since its inception has to make the journey. Once you enter there is no discernible route or progression other than the modern paths you find. You go, enter and surrender, letting it happen.

It is a green place. Green moss on all the stones, tree trunks and paths, and green light sieved through new green leaves. Birdsong claustrophobic and enclosed in the wood. Last night's heavy rain making the stream roar and yet a kind of stillness. The exorcism does not seem quite so daft. It is surely a haunted as well as sacred wood, full of the fantasies that spawned Shakespeare's Bottom and Grimm's tales.

The scale of the sculptures are colossal and astonishing. Two naked giants, twenty feet tall, wrestle in ambiguous congress. A turtle the size of a tank crawls imperceptibly towards the water with the winged figure of Fame on its shell.

A voluptuous reclining giantess, the Donna dormiente, modesty barely covered, is watched over by a little dog, itself the size of a mastiff. She is fleshy, heavy and lovely. A mermaid, two scaly tails akimbo, is as brazenly portrayed as any Sheela na Gig. There is nothing coy here and little decorum. The magic is febrile and disturbing and suggestive of uncontrollable and immeasurable desires.

The most famous piece is the Mouth of Hell, a vast, eye-popping mask whose mouth is the entrance to a cave, complete with an integral table, all big enough for three or four to sit at and look out. This entrance to Hell is light relief and the tourists queue up to have their picture taken within, thumbs up, mouths widely grinning.

The leaning house is more of a puzzle and repels all visitors because the minute you enter eye and brain conflict and the effect is instantaneous sea-sickness. Perhaps that is the joke. Perhaps it symbolises the collapsing House of Orsini, perhaps it is a play on the safety and comfort of house and home. Who knows? From the exterior it is good and witty sculpture and that is enough.

Giulia Farnese died in 1560 and in 1570 Vicino built a temple to her memory at the top of the wood. It is surprisingly conventional and functional and today has a plaque to the memory of Tina Bettini, who died in an accident whilst she was supervising the restoration work of the garden. The floor is covered with bat droppings. It is a sad, sober, rather tender building.

I loved especially the square with its huge urns, presided over at one end by Neptune and flanked by the elephant carrying a wounded warrior in its trunk. The scale sits easily with the trees and rocks and has a balance that is not human. You become a dreamer looking in rather than a mooching tourist looking for entertainment or inspiration for the back garden. Neptune would have once spouted water and the elephant originally carried real tusks and ruby eyes and it seems that all the work may have been brightly painted. Traces remain on the globe carried on top of another gaping, toothy mouth, The Mask of Madness. How different it all must have looked in bright colours and how jarring and brash it would seem like that to our modern eye, in love as we are with the faded tones and textures of weather-worn stone, moss and wood. But that gaudiness would have been entirely consistent with the period, with its love of painted surfaces and decoration.

The place has some disastrous planting with berberis, deodar and Pissard's plum gatecrashing what should be thick, primordial woodland and there is a real need for careful and confident pruning to free vistas and sculptures from pointless tangle. But I think that restoration is unthinkable. Of any garden I have visited this belongs only in your present. To try to understand it is to misunderstand it completely.

Opposite top: A giant tortoise inches towards the Bomarzo castle on the hillside carrying the figure of Fame balancing on a sphere on his shell. There is an engraving made some fifty years after it was carved showing her blowing a double horn. Now she just concentrates on her balance.

Opposite bottom: A dragon attacked by lions is seen beneath the belly of a life-sized elephant carrying a lifeless soldier in its trunk and a turreted castle on its back. Originally the elephant, like all the statues, was brightly painted with real tusks and polished red stones for its eyes.

Above: A lichen-stained herm head carved from the tufa that covers the hillside in great boulders. Many people have tried to understand, interpret and decode Bomarzo but it is unlike any other garden in Italy and remains most potent experienced as strange, haunting and dreamlike.

Tuscany

The Tuscan climate is a fierce one, so its gardens tend to be green, shaded and calm as a relief from the summer heat. Set against the evergreen of box, bay and holm oak, the soft pastels of Mediterranean plants with citrus growing in magnificent terracotta pots are as at home here as anywhere on the planet. But just as the summer heat is astonishing, the winters can be raw and the limonaia used for storing and protecting the citrus plants over winter, that combine the best elements of both chapel and potting shed, are an idiosyncratic necessity.

Since the fifteenth century and the demise of Siena, Florence has dominated Tuscany and the Renaissance, fostered and financed by the Medici dynasty of the fifteenth and sixteenth centuries, was centred there. The roll call of Florentine artists is astonishing. Dante, Giotto, Brunelleschi, Filippo Lippi, Botticelli, Leonardo, Michelangelo and Vasari are merely the better known. No city has such a rich artistic heritage.

The landscape of Renaissance Florence was remarkably similar to modern rural Tuscany – with some highly selective visual editing. Standing above Villa Medici in Fiesole you can look out over the same olive groves, cypresses, orchards and woods today as Lorenzo de' Medici 'il Magnifico' would have seen when he sat in the shade of the loggia discussing philosophy. Now, as then, this is the landscape where the rich and successful make their holiday homes. But, as in Lorenzo's day at the end of the fifteenth century, although wealth is displayed in the countryside, it is made in the city. Although art is condensed and distilled here as nowhere else in earth, Florence's story is one of war, power and the money from banking that made these things possible.

The countryside where today wealthy Germans and British flock to for their holidays existed to service the city, which happily consumed the resulting produce. In Florence that means the Tuscan bread soup ribollita or pinzimonio, a dish of raw vegetables to be dipped in salt and olive oil, followed by the enormous slab of beef that make a bistecca fiorentina.

The garden at Villa Castello, on the outskirts of Florence, is the most faithfully preserved Renaissance garden in Italy. It was made from 1540 by Cosimo de Medici when he was just twenty years old as a relatively cheap way of expressing power and status and impressing visiting statesmen.

It is significant that the most famous food of Siena is panforte, the honied, nutty, spicy cake that is unchangingly medieval. Siena was at its peak in the thirteenth and fourteenth centuries but waned as Florence waxed in the fifteenth century, and in 1557 it succumbed completely to Florentine power and was made part of the Tuscany dukedom. Today Siena is an exquisite medieval city and it is a tribute to Italian sensitivity that it has been allowed to remain fixed at around 1400 yet still vital and in an easy relationship with the twenty-first century. The palio, a horserace around the central Piazza del Campo twice a year between the seventeen regions of the city, is still enacted with real meaning. I was wandering down one of the streets that fan out from the campo when a marshall drumbeat rolled in a crescendo towards me and round the corner came a parade of flag-waving men in medieval costume, all dressed in the plum and blue colours of the Torre contrade. It was wonderful theatre but two things made it very Italian. The first were the serious, handsome faces which were identical to those on the frescoes of the amazing Piccolomini Library in the Duomo painted in 1502. The second was that a few minutes later a fleet of motorbikes swept along a crossing street with the riders all dressed in the green and white colours of the Oca contrade. Both groups did not seem to be so much dressing up as wearing the right clothes for the job. It was for real.

It is hard if not impossible to imagine scenes like this breaking the cool balance of a Luccese afternoon. Lucca remained an independent republic until it was made a principality by Napoleon, with his sister Elisa Bacciochi its princess, and in 1809 it was incorporated into the Grand Duchy of Tuscany with Elisa becoming the grand duchess. Although tiny, the Republic of Lucca was rich, its wealth based upon silk, banking and agriculture with some of the most productive land in Italy. Luccese bankers and merchants built themselves summer houses in the foothills outside the city that, until the seventeenth century, were always working farms. Gradually, as their ambassadors returned from European courts, these farms became elaborate gardens.

The limonaia at Villa La Pietra. Limonaias were large outbuildings, usually with a stove, used to protect the valuable citrus plants during winter and combine all the best qualities of a tithe barn and potting shed. In the foreground is a typical stone plinth for standing a large pot on.

Previous pages: The awkward, sloping site at Castello was levelled to an orderly, gentle slope for the main parterre. The result is simple, ordered and measured. Unlike some preconceptions of formal Renaissance gardens, the formal beds were always filled with flowers and in particular fruit, much of which would be sold to finance the running of the garden. Cosimo was particularly interested in dwarf apple and pear trees and there are currently one hundred and thirty different varieties of citrus plants in over five hundred containers, some of which are huge.

Opposite: The statues and steps of Renaissance gardens have none of the high drama of later baroque gardens. Like these ones here in the lemon garden, they were symbolically important, elegant and reflected the humanist virtues of classicism. Behind them is the limonaia and the bosco above.

Above: In the bosco, above the formal garden, is a reservoir which fed all the fountains and water features below it. In the centre is the statue by Bartolomeo Ammanati from 1540 of the shivering God Appenninus who represents the cold of the Apennine mountains where the Medici family originated from.

Above: The Boboli Gardens – Boboli comes from the name of the Bogoli family from whom the land to make the gardens had originally been bought – were made to display the power of the Medici Dukes, but they now have an exceptional openness and generosity as the city's public park.

Opposite: Throughout the huge garden there are walks and avenues and ragnaia – originally woodland planted as overhanging tunnels which could be netted to catch songbirds – that lead to statues, classical and modern, that fix the eye and entice you down.

Opposite: The gardens are filled with classical statues, many brought from Rome, some original, many copies but all good and all adding to the real sense of privilege that the visitor shares as they freely have access to them set against the backdrop of the gardens.

Top: The grand cypress avenue created a new east-west axis when it was made in the 1630s. It was widened in the eighteenth century to accommodate carriages, removing a labyrinth in the process. It is double-hedged with a low bay hedge topped by a holm oak one running the whole length of the avenue under the cypresses. It was down here that Mussolini and Hitler drove when they met in 1932. *Bottom:* The cypress avenue leads to the isolotto. This originally housed rabbits and chickens for the table, safe within a wide moat, but now is home to flower beds and citrus in pots. The isolotto is not open to the public. The statue of Oceanus in the centre, looking small here but actually huge, once stood in the amphitheatre behind the palace but was moved at the end of the eighteenth century to accommodate the obelisk that is now there.

For years I had pored over the perspective drawings made by J.C. Shepherd on his seminal trip in 1923–25 for the book *Italian Gardens of the Renaissance* with Geoffrey Jellicoe. Jellicoe has always been a profound inspiration and Gamberaia was one of his favourite gardens. So – unwittingly – I had been influenced by Gamberaia in the very earthy reality of my own garden.

This is all hindsight. I don't think I had ever consciously seen a photograph of the place before visiting it. The plan and drawing were such strong icons for me that anything else seemed superfluous. But every image is selective, especially those that mean most to us. To see anything properly, you have to use your own eyes.

One of the reasons that Villa Gamberaia has been so influential over the past hundred years is that it has been relatively easy to visit and see. It is in Settignano, just outside Florence, where Boccaccio lived and where Michelangelo was partly bought up, not far from the Villa I Tatti where Bernard Berenson held court. It also entered the twentieth century relatively unscathed and well tended, compared to many of the Renaissance and baroque gardens of the same period. So if you made the effort to visit, there was something to see that met the expectations of an 'Italian' garden.

It is also completely, perfectly charming – the idealised version of what a Tuscan villa might be. Big enough to impress anyone it is also compact enough to be emulated, at least in part. So it became the model that inspired dozens of other villas and gardens.

The original building was a fourteenth-century convent of Benedictine Nuns and the name comes from a nearby lake where crayfish – gamberi – were caught. Terraces were made on the hillside at the end of the sixteenth century and in 1610 the existing villa was built by Zanobi di Andrea Capo. When he died in 1619, it was passed on to his nephew, Andrea di Lapi, who lived there for sixty years and is believed to have laid out the baroque garden. As with all ambitious baroque gardens, this involved copious supplies of water and, apparently, a legal dispute over water rights that started in 1636 is still rumbling on to this day. But the

greenness of the grass, surrounded by a landscape battered by sun, shows that water is still key to the garden. Andrea di Lapi made the grotto and bowling green and supplied the garden with fountains, ponds, a citrus garden and bosco as well as the expected repertoire of statues, urns and vases, all set on a promontory levelled from the hillside and surrounded with a balustraded stone wall, and bankrupted himself in doing so.

The orchard in front of the house was transformed into an ornate parterre that culminated in a rabbit island like the ones at Boboli and Valsanzibio. In the eighteenth century the garden was owned by the Capponi family, who had other villas around Florence, and they retained it until 1854. Although the house remained lived in and the garden tended, by the end of the nineteenth century the parterre was a kitchen garden which is how Princess Catherine Jeanne Keshko Ghyka and her companion, the splendidly vampiric Joanna Blood, took it on in 1896. People still talk about Princess Ghyka with hushed, reverential tones. The stories of her are highly contradictory. She is recounted as being married but man-hating, a gardener but shunning daylight, a member of the Romanian royal family and a gypsy. She would be seen heavily veiled at a window or glimpsed swimming in her water parterre at night and all this with the distinctly horticultural frisson of lesbian frolics with the aforesaid Miss Blood. There is no way of knowing if any of it is true other than the hard evidence that she loved the place and a great deal of what we see today is a result of her work a hundred years ago, although photographs show that her garden was altogether a sparser place, with more than a touch of Victorian park bedding to it. The rhythms of green on green and volumes of the modern parterre are a result of the changes made after 1924 when it was bought by the American Baroness von Ketteler. In the Second World War the Germans used it as a map depot and headquarters during their retreat from Italy and more or less successfully burned the villa down as they left. It stood as a husk in unkempt gardens for a decade until it was rebuilt and the grounds restored by the Marchi family, who still own it.

As you arrive at the front entrance it is easy to see why it has been idealised. The entrance gates are foursquare, imposing and funnel down a tightly clipped hedge of bulging cypresses. Clipped bulges are always so much more stylish than dead straight. The road tunnels on under a low bridge, which turns out to have been built to carry the full length of the bowling green. The house is unremarkable from the outside, which has the effect of not dominating or controlling the response to the garden. But there are clever tropes to it such as the two flanking arches extended out to match the ones that link the house with the chapel and outhouses, like an abandoned aqueduct. It looks right and proper in that context but is an extraordinarily bold thing.

But boldness is the key and the bowling green at Gamberaia is one of the boldest features in any garden. With hillsides levelled and roads crossed in order to make it, it is flanked by the house and outbuildings on one side and an enormous stuccoed wall on the other. At one end is a nymphaeum with a statue of Neptune at its centre and the other, three hundred full and perfectly flat green yards distant, a pine-fringed, balustraded view over the Tuscan countryside. It is a kind of idealised cityscape, a green city street with buildings and walls as big as buildings on either side topped with trees. It is a completely human space, made for games rather than admiring nature and sets the tone for the garden. It is a very sophisticated version of a football pitch in the back garden.

The parterre hardly reads on an initial, ground-level sighting. That is not to say that it is not pleasing and impressive, but the water is almost lost and the narrative jumbled. But go upstairs to the loggia as I did and look down upon it and it leaps out as a coherent plan built around four large rectangular pools and a much smaller circular pool with a stony fountain in the centre. The size and shape were there in the eighteenth century but Princess Ghyka replaced the ornate parterre de broderie with the water, completely transforming the garden. She also replaced the island at the end with the existing arcaded theatre of cypresses wrapped around a semi-circular pool like an orchestra pit with its ranks of box hedging in front.

Outdoor theatres are a common feature of baroque gardens but at Gamberaia this is all unified in a relatively small space in a particularly pleasing manner. I think that this is because of the way that the Irish yew cones (put in after the Princess left), the blocks and levels of box, the ancient cypress hedge running down one side and the newer cypress arcade, the citrus and pelargoniums in pots (sunk into the hedges) and the lawn running down one side – even the water itself – are all green. There are some unnecessary red roses, but these are a spill rather than a splash of colour. Crouch down and set your eye at hedge level and the clipped greens shape themselves into a deep cubist landscape, or perhaps more accurately that cityscape again, but reduced into a thousand green planes and surfaces. It is an extraordinarily subtle, complex, shifting collage.

Off the bowling green is an entrance to the cabinet di roccaglia, or terrace garden, which is a kind of open-air grotto with steps leading up to the citrus garden. Harold Acton, visiting from La Pietra, described it as "one of the prettiest open-air boudoirs imaginable." Grotto, boudoir, antechamber, you make of it what you will, but on a burning summer afternoon, after the intense green richness of the parterre, it felt abrasive and parched. The huge pots of the citrus garden are laid out on their stone pads set in grassy plats in a grid making a plantation of lemons. If it were your own, you would treasure such a collection and use it as you would use an orchard. But as a visitor there is a tendency simply to compare such formulaic sections of a garden with others you have seen. It is neither fair nor helpful but inevitable. In other words the citrus garden does not define the garden in the way that other parts do. The real action is down below around the house with the deeply satisfying and inspiring bowling green and parterre.

But there is one other touch that gave me huge pleasure from Gamberaia. On the balustrade topping the wall that drops away to the hillside below are wonderful statues of hounds sitting patiently, looking back at the house. Behind them you can see Florence and the Duomo. They have sat there patiently, guarding the household for three hundred years. Good dogs.

Previous pages: On the balustrade of the wall that drops down into the landscape to Florence are statues of hounds. Behind them, you can just see the tower of the Palazzo Vecchio and the Duomo. They have sat there patiently, guarding the household and waiting, for three hundred years.

Above: Looking down from the house to the gates onto the road. The tightly clipped tall cypress hedges bulge and shimmy, but in all the right places, and the minarets of the uncut trees add to the impression of a driveway given the magnificence of a cathedral nave.

Opposite: The bowling green at Gamberaia is astonishingly bold. Over three hundred metres long, with the hillside levelled and a road crossed on the way, it is flanked by the house and outbuildings on one side and an enormous stuccoed wall on the other. At this end is a nymphaeum and at the other a pine-fringed balustraded view over the stunning Tuscan countryside. It is a green, empty street flanked by buildings and walls as big as buildings topped with trees. In other words it is a completely human space, made for entertainment rather than admiring nature.

Above: The green theatre at La Pietra is still used on summer evenings. The performances are timed exactly to catch the best of the evening light, recreating the events of the 1930s which themselves recreated the great performances in the outdoor theatres of seventeenth and eighteenth-century Italian gardens.

Opposite: Although Arthur Acton referred to the garden as a restoration, there was little to restore when he bought it in 1907. So the garden is either a baroque pastiche or a modern creation that perfectly captures the spirit of the villa and place. I tend towards the latter view. An immense amount of statuary and temples, columns, pergolas, pavilions, exedras, steps, balustrades and fountains adorn every area, which in Arthur Acton's day was all for sale, but which now adds to the distinct atmosphere of the garden which is tended with an exceptionally subtle, light hand.